TO

....

WITH LOVE FROM

....

And Keith

HAPPY BIRTHDAY—LOVE . . .

Complete Series

Jane Austen

Joan Crawford

Bette Davis

Liam Gallagher

Audrey Hepburn

John Lennon

Bob Marley

Marilyn Monroe

Michelle Obama

Jackie Kennedy Onassis

Elvis Presley

Keith Richards

Frank Sinatra

Elizabeth Taylor

Oscar Wilde

HAPPY BIRTHDAY
Love, Keith

ON YOUR SPECIAL DAY
ENJOY THE WIT AND WISDOM OF

KEITH RICHARDS

THE HUMAN RIFF

Edited by Jade Riley

CELEBRATION BOOKS

THIS IS A CELEBRATION BOOK

Published by Celebration Books 2023
Celebration Books is an imprint of Dean Street Press

Cover by DSP

ISBN 978 1 915393 74 6

www.deanstreetpress.co.uk

HAPPY BIRTHDAY—LOVE, KEITH

The one and only Keith Richards began life as a working class English boy who fell in love with the guitar and rhythm and blues. It was this love of music and his talent that shot him to stardom and sustained him through a wild journey that most storytellers couldn't even imagine let alone begin to plot. Was it fate or the hand of God that joined him up with Mick Jagger and the rest of the Rolling Stones to create the most legendary of all rock'n'roll bands? Whatever put Keith at the right time and right place to groove and strum for over sixty years is certainly part of the magic that keeps him going.

Who else could survive staying awake for five days to record the album *Some Girls*? Or jump out of a burning house wearing nothing but a T-shirt? Drug busts, tax evasion, electrical shocks, car wrecks, and ejection from the boy scouts are just a smattering of the events in the long history of the outsider bandit that is Keith Richards. Do we wonder that Johnny Depp based his character in *Pirates of the Caribbean* on Keith? Who else, indeed?

Loyal to his art and his wife Patti Hansen, Keith has a loving family with healthy, happy children despite the less than perfect example he may have presented. This multi-millionaire doesn't favor champagne and caviar; the backstage set up for the band is a makeshift English pub with ale, whiskey and a shepherd's pie for dinner. A simple man with simple tastes.

Still Keith knows how lucky he is. The Los Angeles fire where he jumped out the window? All that remained the next day was a chest of drawers with his passport, favorite tapes, jewelry and his gun. "What can I say," he told the journalists, "I'm blessed."

What is life
but playing
with time?

”

Memory is fiction.

”

If you've gotta
think about
being cool,
you ain't cool.

Women are a beautiful complication, and I look forward to far more beauties and far more complications.

You don't find
a style.
A style finds you.

We all have our own personal laboratories. Life is an experiment, and it's just a matter of getting the alchemical or chemical combination right.

Rock and Roll:
Music for
the neck
downwards.

To me, life is a wild animal. You hope to deal with it when it leaps at you.

Fame has killed more very talented guys than drugs. Jimi Hendrix didn't die of an overdose, he died of fame.

Anything you
throw yourself
into, you better
get yourself out of.

It's great to be here. It's great to be anywhere.

If you're going to kick authority in the teeth, you might as well use two feet.

I've never had a
problem with drugs.
I've had problems
with the police.

Everybody thinks you reach a certain age and you're a grownup, but it's not true. Nobody grows up until the day they croak.

You can't accuse me of anything I haven't already confessed to.

Music is a necessity.
After food, air,
water and warmth,
music is the next
necessity of life.

Before Elvis,
everything was in
black and white. Then
came Elvis. Zoom,
glorious Technicolor.

A painter's got a canvas. The writer's got reams of empty paper. A musician has silence.

To me, my biggest fear is getting a big head, and that is when I get the hammer. Because it's very easy in this game to believe you're something special.

My life is full of broken halos.

Give me a guitar,
give me a piano, give
me a broom and
string, I wouldn't get
bored anywhere.

True friends. Hardest thing to find, but you never look for them—they find you; you just grow into each other.

I'm not getting old, I'm evolving.

You don't start to play your guitar thinking you're going to be running an organization that will maybe generate millions.

I've always felt very comfortable on stage, even if I screw up. It always felt like a dog, this is my turf, piss around it.

Why would you want to be anything else if you're Mick Jagger?

It might appear that nothing is happening, but that's actually when it really happens.

I'm an unpure purist, something like that.

We age not by holding
on to youth, but by letting
ourselves grow and
embracing whatever
youthful parts remain.

Art is the last thing I'm worried about when I'm writing a song. As far as I'm concerned, art is just short for 'Arthur.'

Some things get better with age. Like me.

I have never put the make on a girl in my life. I just don't know how to do it. My instincts are always to leave it to the woman.

Everybody's got
a different way of
telling a story—and
has different stories
to tell.

When you are growing up there are two institutional places that affect you most powerfully: the church, which belongs to God, and the public library, which belongs to you.

I'm all for a quiet life. I just didn't get one.

It's called the mysterious rhythm of life, I can't quite account for it. It's probably an addiction, quite honestly. I need that shot of stage every two or three years.

A gut-string classical Spanish guitar, a sweet, lovely little lady. The smell of it. Even now, to open a guitar case, when it's an old wooden guitar, I could crawl in and close the lid.

Nobody wants
to get old, but
nobody wants to
die young either.

The only things
Mick and I disagree
about is the band,
the music and what
we do.

I steal women's clothes.

You get onstage and make other people feel happy. Make them feel good.

I've been through more cold turkeys than there are freezers.

Minimalism has a certain charm.

“

You realized that you were really in one of the sleaziest businesses there is, without actually being a gangster. It was a business where the only time people laughed was when they'd screwed someone else over.

I never thought
I was wasted,
but I probably
was.

I don't encourage anybody to do what I do, you know? Why should you? More for me!

Image is like a long shadow.

“

If you don’t know the blues . . . there’s no point in picking up the guitar and playing rock and roll or any other form of popular music.

Poison's not bad. It's a matter of how much.

Rock and roll ain't nothing but jazz with a hard backbeat.

There's a demon in me, and he's still around. Without the dope, we have a bit more of a chat these days.

Most guys I know are assholes.

”

Everything they'd been brought up not to do, they could do at a rock-and-roll show.

I only get ill when I give up drugs.

I can sustain the impetus over the long tours we do is by feeding off the energy that we get back from an audience. That's my fuel. All I've got is this burning energy, especially when I've got a guitar in my hands.

Rap—so many words, so little said.

Everybody starts by imitating their heroes. For me it was Chuck Berry and Muddy Waters.

To me, the main thing about living on this planet is to know who the hell you are and be real about it. That's the reason I'm still alive.

All the contortions we go through just not to be ourselves for a few hours.

"

I take the view that God, in his infinite wisdom, didn't bother to spring for two joints—heaven and hell.

If you stay up, you get the songs that everyone else misses because they're asleep.

Love has sold
more songs
than you've
had hot dinners.

To write a song that is remembered and taken to heart is a connection, a touching of bases. A thread that runs through all of us. A stab to the heart.

“

I don’t trust doctors. It’s not to say there ain’t some good ones, but on a general level, no, I wouldn’t trust ’em at all.

The big rules of knife fighting are (a) do not try it at home, and (b) the whole point is never, ever use the blade.

“

Great songs write themselves. You’re just being led by the nose, or the ears. The skill is not to interfere with it too much. Ignore intelligence, ignore everything; just follow it where it takes you.

I look for ambiguity
when I'm writing
because life is
ambiguous.

If you're gonna get wasted, get wasted elegantly.

You see, to me, the art of music is listening to it, not playing it.

Songs are strange things. Little notes like that. If they stick, they stick.

I'd rather clean up before I went on the road. It's bad enough cleaning up by yourself, but the idea of putting the whole tour on the line because I couldn't make it was too much; even for me.

Preaching is tax free. Very little to do with God, a lot to do with money.

When you've got three thousand chicks in front of you that are ripping off their panties and throwing them at you, you realize what an awesome power you have unleashed.

Music works in mysterious ways. Once it goes in you have no idea what it can do to you.

You've got the sun, you've got the moon, and you've got the Rolling Stones.

It's a privilege just to wake up to a new day.

And you listen to some of that meticulous Mozart stuff and Vivaldi and you realize that they knew that too. They knew when to leave one note just hanging up there where it illegally belongs and let it dangle in the wind and turn a dead body into a living beauty.

Mick and I may not be friends—too much wear and tear for that—but we're the closest of brothers, and that can't be severed.

How many times I've turned round behind the amplifiers and chucked up, you wouldn't believe!

I mean, some doctor told me I had six months to live and I went to their funeral.

No one's ever going to find out if I had my blood changed or not.

I've got nothing against daylight. I don't live totally nocturnally. Only when I feel like it. Which is most of the time.

I don't
regret
nuthin'.

"The power of the teenage females of thirteen, fourteen, fifteen, when they're in a gang, has never left me. They nearly killed me. I was never more in fear for my life than I was from teenage girls.

“

I’m not putting death on the agenda. I don’t want to see my old friend Lucifer just yet. He’s the guy I’m gonna see, isn’t it? I’m not going to the Other Place, let’s face it.

We are not old men. We are not worried about petty morals.

ABOUT THE EDITOR

JADE Riley is a writer whose interests include old movies, art history, vintage fashion and books, books, books.

Her dream is to move to London, to write like Virginia Woolf, and to meet a man like Mr. Darcy, who owns a vacation home in Greece.

Made in the USA
Middletown, DE
20 September 2023